The Hug of the American People

The HUG of the
AMERICAN
PEOPLE

PRESIDENT
DONALD TRUMP'S
SUPER FAN

GENE HUBER

LIBERTY HILL PUBLISHING

Liberty Hill Publishing
2301 Lucien Way #415
Maitland, FL 32751
407.339.4217
www.libertyhillpublishing.com

New International Version (NIV) Holy Bible, New International
Version®, NIV® Copyright ©1973, 1978, 1984, 2011 by Biblica, Inc.®
Used by permission. All rights reserved worldwide.Printed in the
United States of America.

Edited by Xulon Press.

Printed in the United States of America.

ISBN-13: 978-1-5456-7431-4

Table of Contents

Chapter 1

Who Is Gene Huber?

I was born on January 14, 1970 in Hicksville, New York, Long Island. I have been married to Cathy Huber since 1998. We have two beautiful children, Alyssa, who is eighteen and Gene who is eight years old. I have worked in the supermarket business from my twenties until I was thirty-four years old, then I did ten years in the banking industry. I started as a teller. Then I was a personal banker, and eventually a supervisor on the teller line. I also worked for the U.S. Post Office for one year. Now I'm a car salesman and I work for a friend of mine I grew up with in New York. In fact, I've known him since the second grade. He sells used cars in New York. Even though I live in Florida, I use the Internet to send out pictures of our cars. My job is to get the folks over to that shop in New York to buy our vehicles. He has been in business for twenty-five years now.

My wife owns a preschool that has about ninety kids. It's a very nice facility and she's been running the business for over fifteen years.

I graduated from high school in 1988. When I was in the eleventh grade, my parents decided to move out of New York where I grew up and had lived for seventeen plus years and move to Florida for my last year of high school. That was not good. I had a hard time for the whole year because going from a Long Island high school to Florida was like I had moved to the moon. I didn't know anybody. From high school, I basically went right into the workforce. I started at the bottom in the supermarket business and worked my way up until I was thirty-four.

I always enjoyed sports. I played baseball, basketball, and football all in to high school. I also took up the game of bowling in 1990 and to this present day, I have six, 300 perfect games. My high three game series in bowling is a 786. I hope I can achieve an 800 series in bowling which is almost better than a 300-perfect game. Bowling runs in the family. My father bowls n fact we are very athletic family. My daughter has played girls' fast pitch softball since she was seven years old and all the way up into high school. My son plays baseball and soccer. They are his two favorite sports.

Family is love. Family is being together and having time with each other, whether it's doing homework or kicking a soccer ball with my son or going to my daughter's softball games, it's about togetherness. Love is the most important thing.

I want people to understand after reading this book, God is real. The hug is the hug of the American people. President Trump is the man of the people and leads the way. We will never lose. We will battle, but never lose the fight.

This was the birth of Super Fan as well. I lived, I presently now live in Boynton Beach, Florida, since 1994.

My Faith

Payne Stewart always had this yellow band that said, "WWJD - What Would Jesus Do?" I would hear my father say that when I was growing up. When asked him if something was right or wrong, my dad would ask me if it is good to do then do it but if it is not then don't do it. Now I look at what he taught me as WWJD. When I watched the celebration of Payne Steward's life and his going to heaven service at the church, how everyone spoke about God.[1] I just felt the Holy Spirit leading me to a deeper relationship with the Lord. I pray constantly. I talk to the Lord on a daily basis.

The first thing I do right when I opened up my eyes in the morning is get down on my knees and say, "Good morning, God. Good morning, Jesus. Good morning, Holy Spirit. Good morning ministering angels."

I then read one of my favorite scriptures like Isaiah 40:31 which says, "Those who hope in the Lord, will renew their strength. They will soar on wings like eagles, they will run and not grow weary, they will walk and not faint" (NIV). After I do that, while I'm on my knees, I recite the beautiful Lord's Prayer.

> *Our Father in heaven, hallowed be your name, your kingdom come, your will be done on earth as it is in heaven. Give us this day our daily bread. Forgive our debts, as we also have forgiven our debtors.*

---

[1] See report on his funeral at the end of this book and read about Payne Stewart's spiritual journey that so impacted my life.

And lead us not into temptation, but deliver us from evil, for yours is the kingdom, and the power, and the glory forever. Amen. (Matthew 6:9-13 NIV)

Then I'm ready to start my day. There are times I get attacked just like everyone else by the evil one, but I know what to do. I say, "In the name of Jesus, Satan get behind me." In James 4:7-8 it says, "Submit yourselves, then to God. Resist the devil, and he will flee from you. Come near to God and he will come near to you" (NIV). It just clears my mind because I know my mind is focused on the Lord and that gets any negative thinking out of my brain quickly. It is such a blessing to talk and have a relationship with God.

However, faith without works is dead. You just can't wake up and say, "Alright, God, I know you love me, so let's go." No, you've got to love Him and give Him thanks and show that in all you do all day long. Of course, we're human. The flesh gets us in trouble. The tongue gets us in trouble, but if our relationship is solid with the Lord, He knows our heart. I often pray Psalm 51:10, "Create in me a pure heart, O God, and renew a steadfast spirit within me" (NIV). Jesus says that out of the heart, the mouth speaks (Matthew 12:34). If a person is always complaining, always miserable, they need to fill their heart with thankfulness to God for what He has provided in their lives. We all complain in life at times, but when we begin to focus on all the blessings God has given us, our words will begin to reflect our love and faith in Him. This is a journey that we're on and we need to be constantly growing in faith and love.

Jesus said, "Love the Lord your God with all you heart and with all your soul and with all your mind. This is the first and greatest commandment. And the second is like it: 'You're your neighbor as yourself'" (Matthew 22:37-39 NIV).

Jesus also said, "Love your enemies and pray for those who persecute you" (Matthew 5:44 NIV), so I pray for our enemies. Ever since I've become a "Bullet Superfan" and went live in front of people, I always wrap up my shows saying we have got to pray for everybody.

Chapter 2
Super Fan

NEWS

TRUMP INVITES SUPERFAN ON STAGE DURING RALLY

By Aaron Short

Trump superfan Gene Huber called his embrace of the president the *"moment of his life."*

Huber got to Orlando Melbourne International Airport at 4 a.m. Saturday to be the first person in line *for Trump's rally. Turns out a television interview he gave while online had caught Trump's attention.*

"That's my guy right there. Let him up," Trump said, pointing to Huber midway through his speech. "It's OK. I'm only worried he's going to give me a kiss. I'm not worried about him. Come up here, hop over the fence. Look at him, look at this guy. This guy is great," Trump continued. "Say a couple of words."

Huber shook his head in disbelief and thanked the president.

When Trump took the microphone back, he proclaimed, "A star is born."

My attitude about voting and being politically involved was zero. I had no interest whatsoever in even listening to all the candidates' speeches as they made their bids to enter the presidential race. My attitude was it's the same old stuff we hear them say to us. I would vote for the president every four years, voted for the Republican, and then went to McDonald's for breakfast because I had no interest at all in what was going on with our government.

When President Trump announced he was running for president and he came down the escalator with Melania in Trump Tower in New York, I was clapping. I was starting to feel my energy slowly growing. I knew we were going to have the best president in history.[2]

> "We will be one people, under one God, saluting one American flag."
> – President Donald Trump

---

[2] Read Donald Trump's announcement to run for president at the end of this book.

BOYNTON MAN ON TAKING STAGE WITH TRUMP: 'IT'S STILL A DREAM COME TRUE'

By Aric Chokey
FEB 21, 2017 | 7:05 PM

Donald Trump singled him out and got him to excitedly run up to the stage during a weekend rally at Orlando Melbourne International Airport.

Back home in his Boynton Beach condo, Gene Huber is reminiscing about what he considers a dream come true: Being called onto a stage in front of thousands to meet the president.

Donald Trump singled him out and got him to excitedly run up to the stage during a weekend rally at Orlando Melbourne International Airport.

"It's still a dream come true," Huber said Tuesday. "It's almost like it's not even real."

Since his moment of fame, the 47-year-old married father of two has bounced between interviews with news outlets and said he hopes to use it as a way to advocate for Trump.

Huber, who said he works from home as a car salesman for a company he co-owns, got on board with Trump right after he heard the candidate announce his run. He and his wife were both drawn to Trump's message of being a political outsider, saying they never felt like they trusted politicians.

Huber became so enthusiastic about Trump that he bought a life-size cardboard cutout of him. Every morning, Huber gets out of bed and starts his day by saluting the cutout of Trump, he said.

"I say, 'Good morning Mr. President. I pray for your safety and I want to thank you for your service and have a great day today,'" Huber said.

For the Melbourne rally, Huber set up camp nearly 12 hours ahead of the 3 p.m. event to beat out the estimated 9,000 who attended, he said.

"I sat all by myself on the sidewalk for about an hour and a half," Huber said. "That was my goal and my mission."

Huber managed to be the first in line. During the rally, Trump told the crowd that he had seen Huber on TV because news outlets interviewed him for being at the head of the line.

"That's my guy right there," Trump told the crowd right before calling up Huber.

Once Huber was on stage, they hugged. Huber's daughter, Alyssa, 17, has been excited about seeing her father's name in news headlines, Huber's wife, Cathy, recalled Tuesday. Gene Jr., 5, hasn't really grasped what is going on, she said.

Gene Huber has watched just about every speech Trump has made and has tried to make every local rally since the beginning of his run, his wife said.

But it took three tries for him to get in line. For a rally in West Palm Beach last year, Huber was sixth in line, he said. For Trump's post-election tour stop in Orlando in December, he was third, he said.

Huber said he started paying more attention to current events after starting to support Trump.

"In two years, Donald Trump taught me everything," Huber said. "Just

understanding what's going on in the world. It's just totally bonkers."

While also pro-Trump, Huber's wife said she has been more cautious about discussing her support.

Cathy said she has had to watch who she adds as a friend on social media and grapples with the negative messages her husband has gotten since this weekend.

"It's been really hard," Cathy Huber said. "It's almost like you have to be secret. There's some real not nice people out there."

Gene Huber's Twitter page *swelled from about 130 followers before his stage appearance, to more than 12,000 as of Tuesday afternoon.*

"For me to see some of the comments ... I look at it and want to respond," she said. "[Gene] doesn't care. He looks for the positivity and support and I think he's on the right track."

The attention hasn't yet stopped: Gene Huber has interviews scheduled with news outlets throughout the week after having already been featured on CNN, Fox News and other networks.

Since becoming president last month, Trump made three back-to-back weekend visits to South Florida. Huber said he's looking forward to Trump's next visit.

He hadn't received any follow-up news on Trump's schedule, but he said he has been scanning social media for any hint of another stop.

"As soon as I find out there's a rally, I'm going," Huber said. "Whenever he wants to come on down, we can go get a cocktail or something."

PRESIDENT TRUMP BRINGS MAGA MOVEMENT SUPPORTER GENE HUBER ON STAGE

Posted on February 18, 2017 by sundance

The Peoples' President supporter Gene Huber arrived at 4:00 a.m. to be the first in line to attend the Donald Trump MAGA rally today in Melbourne, Florida. During his speech President Trump noticed Mr. Huber from an earlier TV broadcast and called him onto the stage.

TRUMP TURNS SUPPORTER GENE HUBER INTO 2017'S 'JOE THE PLUMBER'

Published Sat, Feb 18, 2017
Javier E. David

A political star for the masses has been born — or perhaps reborn.

In a blistering campaign-style speech on Saturday, President Donald Trump once again assailed the media while attempting to defend his policy priorities. In an impromptu moment, Trump introduced the world to Gene

Huber, a passionate Trump supporter who claimed to have been waiting in line since the wee hours of Saturday morning for the rally to begin.

Huber, who in a television appearance openly confessed to having regular conversations with a cardboard cutout of the president, immediately launched into a defense of Trump. His appearance also took on a life of its own on social media, with legions of other Trump backers rising to his defense. Trump may have inadvertently anointed 2017's version of Samuel J. Wurzelbacher — otherwise known as Joe the Plumber — a voter who became an unlikely conservative working class hero during the 2008 campaign.

Wurzelbacher backed GOP Arizona senator John McCain's presidential bid, but rocketed to fame after having a confrontation with then-Democratic contender Barack Obama. Wurzelbacher, who moved on to become a grassroots activist, told Reuters in an interview prior to the election that he believed Trump could be successful in the White House.

One of the fixtures of Trump's insurgent campaign was the real estate mogul's rhetorical embrace of the working class, coupled with a stated rejection of cultural elites. Huber appeared to fit the mold of an every-man receptive to Trump's anti-establishment message.

A STAR IS BORN

(https://heavy.com/news/2017/02/gene-huber-donald-trump-rally-melbourne-florida-star-is-born-supporter-video-facebook-twitter-plant/)

It all started with the president looking out into the crowd at his rally and saying, "Look at this guy. Look at this guy. This guy is great. …Come on up. Come here."

The supporter ran on stage and Trump hugged him. Huber, who was wearing a President Donald Trump T-shirt, took the microphone and said, "Mr. President, thank you, sir. We the people, our movement is the reason why our president of the United States is standing here in front of us today. When President Trump during the election promised all these things that he was going to do for us, I knew he was going to do this for us."

Trump shook his hand.

"Mr. President, thank you so much sir," Huber said.

Huber has a Twitter page at @Squeakey6. His profile reads, "Donald J Trump, changed America!" On CNN, Huber said he likes Trump because "he speaks the truth" and he "speaks from his heart."

"There's never been a movement like this ever," he said. "I've never been into politics in my life until President Trump."

In fact, his page is basically an homage or shrine to Trump. He doesn't post about much else.

"This guy," the president said. "So, he's been all over television saying the best things, and I see him standing. Didn't you get here at 4 in the morning? Say a couple of words to this crowd."

TRUMP STOPPED HIS SPEECH TO INVITE ONE OF HIS SUPPORTERS

Up On Stage With Him

*Salvador Hernandez BuzzFeed News Reporter
Posted on February 18, 2017*

President Donald Trump paused in the middle of his speech during a rally in Florida and suddenly invited a supporter up on stage Saturday after recognizing the man from television.

Gene Huber had apparently been the first person in line to a rally in Melbourne, Florida, that drew more than 9,000 supporters Saturday. He had given multiple inter-views to reporters covering the event, seemingly catching the attention of the president.

"Look at this guy, c'mon!" Trump said, pointing at Huber. "Hop over the fence, come on, he can do it."

The seemingly impromptu invitation to stand along with the 45th president seemed to catch the Secret Service off-guard — for a few seconds they appeared to block Huber's path as he tried to make his way up on stage.

"Don't worry about him," Trump said.

Huber than ran to Trump and hugged him.

"Say a couple of words to this crowd," Trump told Huber.

Huber was wearing a black T-shirt with an image of the president on it, and at one point raised his hands up in the air along with Trump.

"We the people, our movement, is the reason why our president is standing here today," Huber said. "I knew he was going to do this for us."

Huber had done several interviews with reporters before the rally, saying it was an "honor" to be the first person standing in line.

"A star is born," Trump said as Huber left the stage.

Huber said he had been standing in line since 4 a.m.

"I want to tell you something, it was the moment of my life," Huber told CNN after the encounter. "I will never ever, ever forget what just happened."

Huber said he has been a big supporter of Trump for two years during he which he had been "fighting battles in and out of lies and terrible things always said about him."

"But we stuck together and it is just an amazing feeling," he said. "He said that he loves me, and I love him, with all my heart."

Huber said he was such a big fan of Trump's that he has a six-foot cardboard cutout of the president at his home.

"I salute that every single day," he said. "And I pray and tell him, 'Mr. President, I pray for your safety today.'"

He also credited Trump for getting him interested in politics.

"He taught me everything," he said.

Chapter 3

President Donald Trump's Impact on My Life

W hat has impacted my life leading up to the election was President Trump's heart of love and truth and how he brings people together like a family. That feeling is a wonderful one because it's God's work. The most important thing I learned before the election was Donald Trump speaks to us. I knew he would do the best for every American – end of story.

"In America, we don't worship government. We worship God."
– President Donald Trump

The Inauguration Speech

President Donald Trump's Inaugural Speech
(CNN) As prepared for delivery

Chief Justice Roberts, President Carter, President Clinton, President Bush, President Obama, fellow Americans, and people of the world: Thank you.

We, the citizens of America, are now joined in a great national effort to rebuild our country and to restore its promise for all of our people.

Together, we will determine the course of America and the world for years to come.

We will face challenges. We will confront hardships. But we will get the job done.

Every four years, we gather on these steps to carry out the orderly and peaceful transfer of power, and we are grateful to President Obama and First Lady Michelle Obama for their gracious aid throughout this transition. They have been magnificent.

Today's ceremony, however, has very special meaning. Because today we are not merely transferring power from one administration to another, or from one party to another – but we are transferring power from Washington, D.C. and giving it back to you, the American People.

Words from the past: Inauguration speech library:

For too long, a small group in our nation's Capital has reaped the rewards of government while the people have borne the cost. Washington flourished – but the people did not share in its wealth. Politicians prospered – but the jobs left, and the factories closed.

The establishment protected itself, but not the citizens of our country. Their victories have not been your victories; their triumphs have not been your triumphs; and while they celebrated in our nation's capital, there was little to celebrate for struggling families all across our land.

That all changes – starting right here, and right now, because this moment is your moment: it belongs to you.

It belongs to everyone gathered here today and everyone watching all across America. This is your day. This is your celebration. And this, the United States of America, is your country.

What truly matters is not which party controls our government, but whether our government is controlled by the people. January 20th 2017, will be remembered as the day the people became the rulers of this nation again. The forgotten men and women of our country will be forgotten no longer.

Everyone is listening to you now.

You came by the tens of millions to become part of a historic movement the likes of which the world has never seen before. At the center of this movement is a crucial conviction: that a nation exists to serve its citizens.

Americans want great schools for their children, safe neighborhoods for their families, and good jobs for themselves. These are the just and reasonable demands of a righteous public.

But for too many of our citizens, a different reality exists: Mothers and children trapped in poverty in our inner cities; rusted-out factories scattered like tombstones across the landscape of our nation; an education system flush with cash, but which leaves our young and beautiful students deprived of knowledge; and the crime and gangs and drugs that have stolen too many lives and robbed our country of so much unrealized potential.

This American carnage stops right here and stops right now.

We are one nation – and their pain is our pain. Their dreams are our dreams; and their success will be our success. We share one heart, one home, and one glorious destiny.

The oath of office I take today is an oath of allegiance to all Americans.

For many decades, we've enriched foreign industry at the expense of American industry; subsidized the armies of other countries while allowing for the very sad depletion of our military; we've defended other nation's borders while refusing to defend our own; and spent trillions of dollars overseas while America's infrastructure has fallen into disrepair and decay.

We've made other countries rich while the wealth, strength, and confidence of our country has disappeared over the horizon.

One by one, the factories shuttered and left our shores, with not even a thought about the millions upon millions of American workers left behind.

The wealth of our middle class has been ripped from their homes and then redistributed across the entire world.

But that is the past. And now we are looking only to the future. We assembled here today are issuing a new decree to be heard in every city, in every foreign capital, and in every hall of power.

From this day forward, a new vision will govern our land.

From this moment on, it's going to be America First.

Every decision on trade, on taxes, on immigration, on foreign affairs, will be made to benefit American workers and American families. We must protect our borders from the ravages of other countries making our products, stealing our companies, and destroying our jobs. Protection will lead to great prosperity and strength.

I will fight for you with every breath in my body – and I will never, ever let you down.

America will start winning again, winning like never before.

We will bring back our jobs. We will bring back our borders. We will bring back our wealth. And we will bring back our dreams.

We will build new roads, and highways, and bridges, and airports, and tunnels, and railways all across our wonderful nation.

We will get our people off of welfare and back to work – rebuilding our country with American hands and American labor.

We will follow two simple rules: Buy American and hire American.

We will seek friendship and goodwill with the nations of the world – but we do so with the understanding that it is the right of all nations to put their own interests first.

We do not seek to impose our way of life on anyone, but rather to let it shine as an example for everyone to follow.

We will reinforce old alliances and form new ones – and unite the civilized world against radical Islamic terrorism, which we will eradicate completely from the face of the Earth.

At the bedrock of our politics will be a total allegiance to the United States of America, and through our loyalty to our country, we will rediscover our loyalty to each other.

When you open your heart to patriotism, there is no room for prejudice. The Bible tells us, "How good and pleasant it is when God's people live together in unity."

We must speak our minds openly, debate our disagreements honestly, but always pursue solidarity.

When America is united, America is totally unstoppable.

There should be no fear – we are protected, and we will always be protected.

We will be protected by the great men and women of our military and law enforcement and, most importantly, we are protected by God.

Finally, we must think big and dream even bigger.

In America, we understand that a nation is only living as long as it is striving.

We will no longer accept politicians who are all talk and no action – constantly complaining but never doing anything about it.

The time for empty talk is over. Now arrives the hour of action.

Do not let anyone tell you it cannot be done. No challenge can match the heart and fight and spirit of America.

We will not fail. Our country will thrive and prosper again.

We stand at the birth of a new millennium, ready to unlock the mysteries of space, to free the Earth from the miseries of disease, and to harness the energies, industries and technologies of tomorrow.

A new national pride will stir our souls, lift our sights, and heal our divisions.

It is time to remember that old wisdom our soldiers will never forget: that whether we are black or brown or white, we all bleed the same red blood of patriots, we all enjoy the same glorious freedoms, and we all salute the same great American Flag.

And whether a child is born in the urban sprawl of Detroit or the windswept plains of Nebraska, they look up at the same night sky, they fill their heart with the same dreams, and they are infused with the breath of life by the same almighty Creator.

So to all Americans, in every city near and far, small and large, from mountain to mountain, and from ocean to ocean, hear these words:

You will never be ignored again.

Your voice, your hopes, and your dreams will define our American destiny. And your courage and goodness and love will forever guide us along the way.

Together, We will make America strong again.

We will make wealthy again.

We will make America proud again.

We will make America safe again.

And yes, together, we will make America great again.

Thank you. God bless you. And God bless America.

The impact on the day of his inauguration speech came from listening and watching carefully and telling God thank you for a leader who loves us, The People. The day he was elected, the world changed for me and my fellow Americans. This President tells us we do this together. He truly makes me feel what it means to be a true American. Whatever President Trump tells us, I support him 100 percent of the time.

"Our republic was formed on the basis that freedom is not a gift from government, but that freedom is a gift from God."

– President Donald Trump

I have been to fourteen rallies front and center with President Trump hearing him talk directly to us, the feeling you have being ten steps away from him and hearing him talk to us. The rallies are in a sense the same, but each one has more accomplishments that he has done as President. He tells us everything he is doing, fixing, and all his promises kept, that our saying he brings positivity and love and the family atmosphere, and we all feel loved. I learned everything from how this country and world should be run by a leader like President Trump and he is a father figure to me. He is my hero.

President Trump's Cabinet Praying Before Their Meeting
President Trump knows the Power of Prayer!

October 13, 2016 – My first rally Palm Beach County Fairgrounds
January 2017 – Thank you tour rally Orlando, Florida
February 18, 2017 – Melbourne, Florida (The day of The Hug)
April 29, 2017 – Harrisburg, Pennsylvania
June 21, 2017 – Cedar Rapids, Iowa
July 25, 2017 – Youngstown, Ohio
August 3, 2017 – Huntington, West Virginia
August 22, 2017 – Phoenix, Arizona
December 9, 2017 – Pensacola, Florida
March 10, 2018 – Moon Township, Pennsylvania
July 31, 2018 – Tampa, Florida
October 13, 2018 – Richmond, Kentucky
October 31, 2018 – Ft. Meyers, Florida
April 27, 2019 – Green Bay, Wisconsin
March 23, I went to cheer the presidential motorcade as it traveled
to and from Mar-a-Lago.

"As long as we have God, we are never, ever alone.
Whether it's the soldier on night watch, or the single parent on
the night shift,
God will always give us solace and strength, and comfort."
– President Donald Trump

Since the day of the hug until today, I treat my show like a President Trump rally. We bring love, smiles, and we bring people together. I go to the bridge when he arrives in Florida to wave and show love and support. My forty thousand plus followers on social media see the pictures of President Trump and his family and show the love and support I have for him and the people. I go to local events when I can. I call into a Fox Radio station once a month called The Todd Starnes Show. I use any way I can to get my voice out there to tell the world I love President Trump and to show him love and support.

My Show

My way with being super fan, I always say on my shows and I'm doing interviews, I say, "We have got to have a love for the people." Our President has taught me a lot about the family and the love and unite as one. When I was young, I always thought about how athletes are able to touch people's lives with the things they do. People know who they are in the world. I've always said that if I can make one person laugh, that makes me very happy. I want people to say, you know that man, Gene, he has put a smile on my face. I could have had the worst day in the world, but I knew I was going to watch Gene's show and he was going to make me laugh or make me feel confident. I just want people to know I am there for them to make their lives better in some way.

My Message to President Trump

President Trump, what I've seen from you from the get go is showing us God, family, love, and we are united as one. You're the Messenger, so you'll be an example to all of us Americans. We believe in you because we know that you're a praying man, you believe in God, and you understand we worship God and not the government. We understand, Mr. President, that when you wake up every morning you are prepared to work for the people of this country. Everything you say is about what we can all do to make

America Great Again! When we watch you at rallies, on Twitter, and on TV, you talk about us and you always tell us it's about the "we" and that brings us together.

Our President is a seventy-year-old billionaire. He did not have to take on this job as President of the United States, but God said it's time for a man that has a heart of love for this country and who believes in God to have this position. Past government leaders wanted to take God out of the government. Now they're in trouble because they did the wrong things in God's eyes for way too long. They could have stopped, they could have done the right things for the people, but you came aboard, Mr. President, with the love in your heart to show us what we can do together. I thank you so much for showing each person that you care about them.

Appendix 1
Videos

Here is the video where Trump calls him up: https://www.youtube.com/watch?v=4WUkbjpkLAQ

Here he is outside of Mar-a-Lago (Trumps home) being interviewed by the Washington Post: https://www.youtube.com/watch?v=T3eqz4lZoxg He is the guy with the face of Trump on his shirt.

Trump fans gathered near a bridge in West Palm Beach, Fla., on March 23, to cheer the presidential motorcade as it traveled to and from Mar-a-Lago. Read more: https://wapo.st/2WlLd4q.

Appendix 2

Donald Trump Announces He Will run for President of the United States By TIME Staff

JUNE 16, 2015

Wow. Whoa. That is some group of people. Thousands.

So nice, thank you very much. That's really nice. Thank you. It's great to be at Trump Tower. It's great to be in a wonderful city, New York. And it's an honor to have everybody here. This is beyond anybody's expectations. There's been no crowd like this.

And, I can tell, some of the candidates, they went in. They didn't know the air-conditioner didn't work. They sweated like dogs.

They didn't know the room was too big, because they didn't have anybody there. How are they going to beat ISIS? I don't think it's gonna happen.

Our country is in serious trouble. We don't have victories anymore. We used to have victories, but we don't have them. When was the last time anybody saw us beating, let's say, China in a trade deal? They kill us. I beat China all the time. All the time.

When did we beat Japan at anything? They send their cars over by the millions, and what do we do? When was the last time you saw a Chevrolet in Tokyo? It doesn't exist, folks. They beat us all the time.

When do we beat Mexico at the border? They're laughing at us, at our stupidity. And now they are beating us economically. They are not our friend, believe me. But they're killing us economically.

The U.S. has become a dumping ground for everybody else's problems.

Thank you. It's true, and these are the best and the finest. When Mexico sends its people, they're not sending their best. They're not sending you. They're not sending you. They're sending people that have lots of problems, and they're bringing those problems with us. They're bringing drugs. They're bringing crime. They're rapists. And some, I assume, are good people.

But I speak to border guards and they tell us what we're getting. And it only makes common sense. It only makes common sense. They're sending us not the right people.

It's coming from more than Mexico. It's coming from all over South and Latin America, and it's coming probably— probably— from the Middle East. But we don't know. Because we have no protection and we have no competence, we don't know what's happening. And it's got to stop and it's got to stop fast.

Islamic terrorism is eating up large portions of the Middle East. They've become rich. I'm in competition with them.

They just built a hotel in Syria. Can you believe this? They built a hotel. When I have to build a hotel, I pay interest. They don't have to pay interest, because they took the oil that, when we left Iraq, I said we should've taken.

So now ISIS has the oil, and what they don't have, Iran has. And in 19— and I will tell you this, and I said it very strongly, years ago, I said— and I love the military, and I want to have the strongest military that we've ever had, and we need it more now than ever. But I said, "Don't hit Iraq," because you're going to totally destabilize the Middle East. Iran is going to take over the Middle East, Iran and somebody else will get the oil, and it turned out that Iran is now taking over Iraq. Think of it. Iran is taking over Iraq, and they're taking it over big league.

We spent $2 trillion in Iraq, $2 trillion. We lost thousands of lives, thousands in Iraq. We have wounded soldiers, who I love, I love — they're great — all over the place, thousands and thousands of wounded soldiers.

And we have nothing. We can't even go there. We have nothing. And every time we give Iraq equipment, the first time a bullet goes off in the air, they leave it

Thank you. It's true, and these are the best and the finest. When Mexico sends its people, they're not sending their best. They're not sending you. They're not sending you. They're sending people that have lots of problems, and they're bringing those problems with us. They're bringing drugs. They're bringing crime. They're rapists. And some, I assume, are good people.

But I speak to border guards and they tell us what we're getting. And it only makes common sense. It only makes common sense. They're sending us not the right people.

It's coming from more than Mexico. It's coming from all over South and Latin America, and it's coming probably— probably— from the Middle East. But we don't know. Because we have no protection and we have no competence, we don't know what's happening. And it's got to stop and it's got to stop fast.

Islamic terrorism is eating up large portions of the Middle East. They've become rich. I'm in competition with them.

They just built a hotel in Syria. Can you believe this? They built a hotel. When I have to build a hotel, I pay interest. They don't have to pay interest, because they took the oil that, when we left Iraq, I said we should've taken.

So now ISIS has the oil, and what they don't have, Iran has. And in 19— and I will tell you this, and I said it very strongly, years ago, I said— and I love the military, and I want to have the strongest military that we've ever had, and we need it more now than ever. But I said, "Don't hit Iraq," because you're going to totally destabilize the Middle East. Iran is going to take over the Middle East, Iran and somebody else will get the oil, and it turned out that Iran is now taking over Iraq. Think of it. Iran is taking over Iraq, and they're taking it over big league.

We spent $2 trillion in Iraq, $2 trillion. We lost thousands of lives, thousands in Iraq. We have wounded soldiers, who I love, I love — they're great — all over the place, thousands and thousands of wounded soldiers.

And we have nothing. We can't even go there. We have nothing. And every time we give Iraq equipment, the first time a bullet goes off in the air, they leave it.

Last week, I read 2,300 Humvees— these are big vehicles— were left behind for the enemy. 2,000? You would say maybe two, maybe four? 2,300 sophisticated vehicles, they ran, and the enemy took them.

Last quarter, it was just announced our gross domestic product— a sign of strength, right? But not for us. It was below zero. Whoever heard of this? It's never below zero.

Our labor participation rate was the worst since 1978. But think of it, GDP below zero, horrible labor participation rate.

And our real unemployment is anywhere from 18 to 20 percent. Don't believe the 5.6. Don't believe it.

That's right. A lot of people up there can't get jobs. They can't get jobs, because there are no jobs, because China has our jobs and Mexico has our jobs. They all have jobs.

But the real number, the real number is anywhere from 18 to 19 and maybe even 21 percent, and nobody talks about it, because it's a statistic that's full of nonsense.

Our enemies are getting stronger and stronger by the way, and we as a country are getting weaker. Even our nuclear arsenal doesn't work.

It came out recently they have equipment that is 30 years old. They don't know if it worked. And I thought it was horrible when it was broadcast on television, because boy, does that send signals to Putin and all of the other people that look at us and they say, "That is a group of people, and that is a nation that truly has no clue. They don't know what they're doing. They don't know what they're doing."

We have a disaster called the big lie: Obamacare. Obamacare.

Yesterday, it came out that costs are going for people up 29, 39, 49, and even 55 percent, and deductibles are through the roof. You have to be hit by a tractor, literally, a tractor, to use it, because the deductibles are so high, it's virtually useless. It's virtually useless. It is a disaster.

And remember the $5 billion website? $5 billion we spent on a website, and to this day it doesn't work. A $5 billion website.

I have so many websites, I have them all over the place. I hire people, they do a website. It costs me $3. $5 billion website.

Well, you need somebody, because politicians are all talk, no action. Nothing's gonna get done. They will not bring us— believe me— to the promised land. They will not.

As an example, I've been on the circuit making speeches, and I hear my fellow Republicans. And they're wonderful people. I like them. They all want me to support them. They don't know how to bring it about. They come up to my office. I'm meeting with three of them in the next week. And they don't know— "Are you running? Are you not running? Could we have your support? What do we do? How do we do it?"

I like them. And I hear their speeches. And they don't talk jobs and they don't talk China. When was the last time you heard China is killing us? They're devaluing their currency to a level that you wouldn't believe. It makes it impossible for our companies to compete, impossible. They're killing us.

But you don't hear that from anybody else. You don't hear it from anybody else. And I watch the speeches.

I watch the speeches of these people, and they say the sun will rise, the moon will set, all sorts of wonderful things will happen. And people are saying, "What's going on? I just want a job. Just get me a job. I don't need the rhetoric. I want a job."

And that's what's happening. And it's going to get worse, because remember, Obamacare really kicks in in '16, 2016. Obama is going to be out playing golf. He might be on one of my courses. I would invite him, I actually would say. I have the best courses in the world, so I'd say, you what, if he wants to— I have one right next to the White House, right on the Potomac. If he'd like to play, that's fine.

In fact, I'd love him to leave early and play, that would be a very good thing.

But Obamacare kicks in in 2016. Really big league. It is going to be amazingly destructive. Doctors are quitting. I have a friend who's a doctor, and he said to me the other day, "Donald, I never saw anything like it. I have more accountants than I have nurses. It's a disaster. My patients are beside themselves. They had a plan that was good. They have no plan now."

We have to repeal Obamacare, and it can be— and— and it can be replaced with something much better for everybody. Let it be for everybody. But much better and much less expensive for people and for the government. And we can do it.

So I've watched the politicians. I've dealt with them all my life. If you can't make a good deal with a politician, then there's something wrong with you. You're certainly not very good. And that's what we have representing us. They will never make America great again. They don't even have a chance. They're controlled fully— they're controlled fully by the lobbyists, by the donors, and by the special interests, fully.

Yes, they control them. Hey, I have lobbyists. I have to tell you. I have lobbyists that can produce anything for me. They're great. But you know what? it won't happen.

It won't happen. Because we have to stop doing things for some people, but for this country, it's destroying our country. We have to stop, and it has to stop now.

Now, our country needs— our country needs a truly great leader, and we need a truly great leader now. We need a leader that wrote "The Art of the Deal."

We need a leader that can bring back our jobs, can bring back our manufacturing, can bring back our military, can take care of our vets. Our vets have been abandoned.

And we also need a cheerleader.

You know, when President Obama was elected, I said, "Well, the one thing, I think he'll do well. I think he'll be a great cheerleader for the country. I think he'd be a great spirit."

He was vibrant. He was young. I really thought that he would be a great cheerleader.

He's not a leader. That's true. You're right about that.

But he wasn't a cheerleader. He's actually a negative force. He's been a negative force. He wasn't a cheerleader; he was the opposite.

We need somebody that can take the brand of the United States and make it great again. It's not great again.

We need— we need somebody— we need somebody that literally will take this country and make it great again. We can do that.

And, I will tell you, I love my life. I have a wonderful family. They're saying, "Dad, you're going to do something that's going to be so tough."

You know, all of my life, I've heard that a truly successful person, a really, really successful person and even modestly successful cannot run for public office. Just can't happen. And yet that's the kind of mindset that you need to make this country great again.

So ladies and gentlemen...I am officially running... for president of the United States, and we are going to make our country great again.

It can happen. Our country has tremendous potential. We have tremendous people.

We have people that aren't working. We have people that have no incentive to work. But they're going to have incentive to work, because the greatest social program is a job. And they'll be proud, and they'll love it, and they'll make much more than they would've ever made, and they'll be— they'll be doing so well, and we're going to be thriving as a country, thriving. It can happen.

I will be the greatest jobs president that God ever created. I tell you that.

I'll bring back our jobs from China, from Mexico, from Japan, from so many places. I'll bring back our jobs, and I'll bring back our money.

Right now, think of this: We owe China $1.3 trillion. We owe Japan more than that. So they come in, they take our jobs, they take our money, and then they loan us back the money, and we pay them in interest, and then the dollar goes up so their deal's even better.

How stupid are our leaders? How stupid are these politicians to allow this to happen? How stupid are they?

I'm going to tell you— thank you. I'm going to tell you a couple of stories about trade, because I'm totally against the trade bill for a number of reasons.

Number one, the people negotiating don't have a clue. Our president doesn't have a clue. He's a bad negotiator.

He's the one that did Bergdahl. We get Bergdahl, they get five killer terrorists that everybody wanted over there.

We get Bergdahl. We get a traitor. We get a no-good traitor, and they get the five people that they wanted for years, and those people are now back on the battlefield trying to kill us. That's the negotiator we have.

Take a look at the deal he's making with Iran. He makes that deal, Israel maybe won't exist very long. It's a disaster, and we have to protect Israel. But...

So we need people— I'm a free trader. But the problem with free trade is you need really talented people to negotiate for you. If you don't have talented people, if you don't have great leadership, if you don't have people that know business, not just a political hack that got the job because he made a contribution to a campaign, which is the way all jobs, just about, are gotten, free trade terrible.

Free trade can be wonderful if you have smart people, but we have people that are stupid. We have people that aren't smart. And we have people that are controlled by special interests. And it's just not going to work.

So, here's a couple of stories happened recently. A friend of mine is a great manufacturer. And, you know, China comes over and they dump all their stuff, and I buy it. I buy it, because, frankly, I have an obligation to buy it, because they devalue their currency so brilliantly, they just did it recently, and nobody thought they could do it again.

But with all our problems with Russia, with all our problems with everything— everything, they got away with it again. And it's impossible for our people here to compete.

So I want to tell you this story. A friend of mine who's a great manufacturer, calls me up a few weeks ago. He's very upset. I said, "What's your problem?"

He said, "You know, I make great product."

And I said, "I know. I know that because I buy the product."

He said, "I can't get it into China. They won't accept it. I sent a boat over and they actually sent it back. They talked about environmental, they talked about all sorts of crap that had nothing to do with it."

I said, "Oh, wait a minute, that's terrible. Does anyone know this?"

He said, "Yeah, they do it all the time with other people."

I said, "They send it back?"

"Yeah. So I finally got it over there and they charged me a big tariff. They're not supposed to be doing that. I told them."

Now, they do charge you tariff on trucks, when we send trucks and other things over there.

Ask Boeing. They wanted Boeing's secrets. They wanted their patents and all their secrets before they agreed to buy planes from Boeing.

Hey, I'm not saying they're stupid. I like China. I sell apartments for— I just sold an apartment for $15 million to somebody from China. Am I supposed to dislike them? I own a big chunk of the Bank of America Building at 1290 Avenue of the Americas, that I got from China in a war. Very valuable.

I love China. The biggest bank in the world is from China. You know where their United States headquarters is located? In this building, in Trump Tower. I love China. People say, "Oh, you don't like China?"

No, I love them. But their leaders are much smarter than our leaders, and we can't sustain ourself with that. There's too much— it's like— it's like take the New England Patriots and Tom Brady and have them play your high school football team. That's the difference between China's leaders and our leaders.

They are ripping us. We are rebuilding China. We're rebuilding many countries. China, you go there now, roads, bridges, schools, you never saw anything like it. They have bridges that make the George Washington Bridge look like small potatoes. And they're all over the place.

We have all the cards, but we don't know how to use them. We don't even know that we have the cards, because our leaders don't understand the game. We could turn off that spigot by charging them tax until they behave properly.

Now they're going militarily. They're building a military island in the middle of the South China sea. A military island. Now, our country could never do that because we'd have to get environmental clearance, and the environmentalist wouldn't let our country— we would never build in an ocean. They built it in about one year, this massive military port.

They're building up their military to a point that is very scary. You have a problem with ISIS. You have a bigger problem with China.

And, in my opinion, the new China, believe it or not, in terms of trade, is Mexico.

So this man tells me about the manufacturing. I say, "That's a terrible story. I hate to hear it."

But I have another one, Ford.

So Mexico takes a company, a car company that was going to build in Tennessee, rips it out. Everybody thought the deal was dead. Reported it in the Wall Street Journal recently. Everybody thought it was a done deal. It's going in and that's going to be it, going into Tennessee. Great state, great people.

All of a sudden, at the last moment, this big car manufacturer, foreign, announces they're not going to Tennessee. They're gonna spend their $1 billion in Mexico instead. Not good.

Now, Ford announces a few weeks ago that Ford is going to build a $2.5 billion car and truck and parts manufacturing plant in Mexico. $2.5 billion, it's going to be one of the largest in the world. Ford. Good company.

So I announced that I'm running for president. I would...

... one of the early things I would do, probably before I even got in— and I wouldn't even use— you know, I have— I know the smartest negotiators in the world. I know the good ones. I know the bad ones. I know the overrated ones.

You get a lot of them that are overrated. They're not good. They think they are. They get good stories, because the newspapers get buffaloed. But they're not good.

But I know the negotiators in the world, and I put them one for each country. Believe me, folks. We will do very, very well, very, very well.

But I wouldn't even waste my time with this one. I would call up the head of Ford, who I know. If I was president, I'd say, "Congratulations. I understand that you're building a nice $2.5 billion car factory in Mexico and that you're going to take your cars and sell them to the United States zero tax, just flow them across the border."

And you say to yourself, "How does that help us," right? "How does that help us? Where is that good"? It's not.

So I would say, "Congratulations. That's the good news. Let me give you the bad news. Every car and every truck and every part manufactured in this plant that comes across the border, we're going to charge you a 35-percent tax, and that tax is going to be paid simultaneously with the transaction, and that's it.

Now, here's what is going to happen. If it's not me in the position, it's one of these politicians that we're running against, you know, the 400 people that we're (inaudible). And here's what's going to happen. They're not so stupid. They know it's not a good thing, and they may even be upset by it. But then they're going to get a call from the donors or probably from the lobbyist for Ford and say, "You can't do that to Ford, because Ford takes care of me and I take care of you, and you can't do that to Ford."

And guess what? No problem. They're going to build in Mexico. They're going to take away thousands of jobs. It's very bad for us.

So under President Trump, here's what would happen:

The head of Ford will call me back, I would say within an hour after I told them the bad news. But it could be he'd want to be cool, and he'll wait until the next day. You know, they want to be a little cool.

And he'll say, "Please, please, please." He'll beg for a little while, and I'll say, "No interest." Then he'll call all sorts of political people, and I'll say, "Sorry, fellas. No interest," because I don't need anybody's money. It's nice. I don't need anybody's money.

I'm using my own money. I'm not using the lobbyists. I'm not using donors. I don't care. I'm really rich. I (inaudible).

And by the way, I'm not even saying that's the kind of mindset, that's the kind of thinking you need for this country.

So— because we got to make the country rich.

It sounds crass. Somebody said, "Oh, that's crass." It's not crass.

We got $18 trillion in debt. We got nothing but problems.

We got a military that needs equipment all over the place. We got nuclear weapons that are obsolete.

We've got nothing. We've got Social Security that's going to be destroyed if somebody like me doesn't bring money into the country. All these other people want to cut the hell out of it. I'm not going to cut it at all; I'm going to bring money in, and we're going to save it.

But here's what's going to happen:

After I'm called by 30 friends of mine who contributed to different campaigns, after I'm called by all of the special interests and by the— the donors and by the lobbyists— and they have zero chance at convincing me, zero— I'll get a call the next day from the head of Ford. He'll say. "Please reconsider," I'll say no.

He'll say, "Mr. President, we've decided to move the plant back to the United States, and we're not going to build it in Mexico." That's it. They have no choice. They have no choice.

There are hundreds of things like that. I'll give you another example.

Saudi Arabia, they make $1 billion a day. $1 billion a day. I love the Saudis. Many are in this building. They make a billion dollars a day. Whenever they have problems, we send over the ships. We say "we're gonna protect." What are we doing? They've got nothing but money.

If the right person asked them, they'd pay a fortune. They wouldn't be there except for us.

And believe me, you look at the border with Yemen. You remember Obama a year ago, Yemen was a great victory. Two weeks later, the place was blown up. Everybody got out— and they kept our equipment.

They always keep our equipment. We ought to send used equipment, right? They always keep our equipment. We ought to send some real junk, because, frankly, it would be— we ought to send our surplus. We're always losing this gorgeous brand-new stuff.

But look at that border with Saudi Arabia. Do you really think that these people are interested in Yemen? Saudi Arabia without us is gone. They're gone.

And I'm the one that made all of the right predictions about Iraq. You know, all of these politicians that I'm running against now— it's so nice to say I'm running as opposed to if I run, if I run. I'm running.

But all of these politicians that I'm running against now, they're trying to disassociate. I mean, you looked at Bush, it took him five days to answer the question on Iraq. He couldn't answer the question. He didn't know. I said, "Is he intelligent?"

Then I looked at Rubio. He was unable to answer the question, is Iraq a good thing or bad thing? He didn't know. He couldn't answer the question.

How are these people gonna lead us? How are we gonna— how are we gonna go back and make it great again? We can't. They don't have a clue. They can't lead us. They can't. They can't even answer simple questions. It was terrible.

But Saudi Arabia is in big, big trouble. Now, thanks to fracking and other things, the oil is all over the place. And I used to say it, there are ships at sea, and this was during the worst crisis, that were loaded up with oil, and the cartel kept the price up, because, again, they were smarter than our leaders. They were smarter than our leaders.

There is so much wealth out there that can make our country so rich again, and therefore make it great again. Because we need money. We're dying. We're dying. We need money. We have to do it. And we need the right people.

So Ford will come back. They'll all come back. And I will say this, this is going to be an election, in my opinion, that's based on competence.

Somebody said — thank you, darlin'.

Somebody said to me the other day, a reporter, a very nice reporter, "But, Mr. Trump, you're not a nice person."

That's true. But actually I am. I think I am a nice person. People that know me, like me. Does my family like me? I think so, right. Look at my family. I'm proud of my family.

By the way, speaking of my family, Melania, Barron, Kai, Donnie, Don, Vanessa, Tiffany, Evanka did a great job. Did she do a great job?

Great. Jared, Laura and Eric, I'm very proud of my family. They're a great family.

So the reporter said to me the other day, "But, Mr. Trump, you're not a nice person. How can you get people to vote for you?"

I said, "I don't know." I said, "I think that number one, I am a nice person. I give a lot of money away to charities and other things. I think I'm actually a very nice person."

But, I said, "This is going to be an election that's based on competence, because people are tired of these nice people. And they're tired of being ripped off by everybody in the world. And they're tired of spending more money on education than any nation in the world per capita, than any nation in the world, and we are 26th in the world, 25 countries are better than us in education.

And some of them are like third world countries. But we're becoming a third word country, because of our infrastructure, our airports, our roads, everything. So one of the things I did, and I said, you know what I'll do. I'll do it. Because a lot of people said, "He'll never run. Number one, he won't want to give up his lifestyle."

They're right about that, but I'm doing it.

Number two, I'm a private company, so nobody knows what I'm worth. And the one thing is that when you run, you have to announce and certify to all sorts of governmental authorities your net worth.

So I said, "That's OK." I'm proud of my net worth. I've done an amazing job.

I started off— thank you— I started off in a small office with my father in Brooklyn and Queens, and my father said — and I love my father. I learned so much. He was a great negotiator. I learned so much just sitting at his feet playing with blocks listening to him negotiate with subcontractors. But I learned a lot.

But he used to say, "Donald, don't go into Manhattan. That's the big leagues. We don't know anything about that. Don't do it."

I said, "I gotta go into Manhattan. I gotta build those big buildings. I gotta do it, Dad. I've gotta do it."

And after four or five years in Brooklyn, I ventured into Manhattan and did a lot of great deals— the Grand Hyatt Hotel. I was responsible for the convention center on the west side. I did a lot of great deals, and I did them early and young. And now I'm building all over the world, and I love what I'm doing.

But they all said, a lot of the pundits on television, "Well, Donald will never run, and one of the main reasons is he's private and he's probably not as successful as everybody thinks."

So I said to myself, you know, nobody's ever going to know unless I run, because I'm really proud of my success. I really am.

I've employed— I've employed tens of thousands of people over my lifetime. That means medical. That means education. That means everything.

So a large accounting firm and my accountants have been working for months, because it's big and complex, and they've put together a statement, a financial statement, just a summary. But everything will be filed eventually with the government, and we don't [use] extensions or anything. We'll be filing it right on time. We don't need anything.

And it was even reported incorrectly yesterday, because they said, "He had assets of $9 billion." So I said, "No, that's the wrong number. That's the wrong number. Not assets."

So they put together this. And before I say it, I have to say this. I made it the old-fashioned way. It's real estate. You know, it's real estate.

It's labor, and it's unions good and some bad and lots of people that aren't in unions, and it's all over the place and building all over the world.

And I have assets— big accounting firm, one of the most highly respected— 9 billion 240 million dollars.

And I have liabilities of about $500 million. That's long-term debt, very low interest rates.

In fact, one of the big banks came to me and said, "Donald, you don't have enough borrowings. Could we loan you $4 billion"? I said, "I don't need it. I don't want it. And I've been there. I don't want it."

But in two seconds, they give me whatever I wanted. So I have a total net worth, and now with the increase, it'll be well-over $10 billion. But here, a total net worth of—net worth, not assets, not— a net worth, after all debt, after all expenses, the greatest assets— Trump Tower, 1290 Avenue of the Americas, Bank of America building in San Francisco, 40 Wall Street, sometimes referred to as the Trump building right opposite the New York— many other places all over the world.

So the total is $8,737,540,00.

Now I'm not doing that...

I'm not doing that to brag, because you know what? I don't have to brag. I don't have to, believe it or not.

I'm doing that to say that that's the kind of thinking our country needs. We need that thinking. We have the opposite thinking.

We have losers. We have losers. We have people that don't have it. We have people that are morally corrupt. We have people that are selling this country down the drain.

So I put together this statement, and the only reason I'm telling you about it today is because we really do have to get going, because if we have another three or four years— you know, we're at $8 trillion now. We're soon going to be at $20 trillion.

According to the economists— who I'm not big believers in, but, nevertheless, this is what they're saying— that $24 trillion— we're very close— that's the point of no return. $24 trillion. We will be there soon. That's when we become Greece. That's when we become a country that's unsalvageable. And we're gonna be there very soon. We're gonna be there very soon.

So, just to sum up, I would do various things very quickly. I would repeal and replace the big lie, Obamacare.

I would build a great wall, and nobody builds walls better than me, believe me, and I'll build them very inexpensively, I will build a great, great wall on our southern border. And I will have Mexico pay for that wall.

Mark my words.

Nobody would be tougher on ISIS than Donald Trump. Nobody.

I will find — within our military, I will find the General Patton or I will find General MacArthur, I will find the right guy. I will find the guy that's going to take that military and make it really work. Nobody, nobody will be pushing us around.

I will stop Iran from getting nuclear weapons. And we won't be using a man like Secretary Kerry that has absolutely no concept of negotiation, who's making a horrible and laughable deal, who's just being tapped along as they make weapons right now, and then goes into a bicycle race at 72 years old, and falls and breaks his leg. I won't be doing that. And I promise I will never be in a bicycle race. That I can tell you.

I will immediately terminate President Obama's illegal executive order on immigration, immediately.

Fully support and back up the Second Amendment.

Now, it's very interesting. Today I heard it. Through stupidity, in a very, very hard core prison, interestingly named Clinton, two vicious murderers, two vicious people escaped, and nobody knows where they are. And a woman was on television this morning, and she said, "You know, Mr. Trump," and she was telling other people, and I actually called her, and she said, "You know, Mr. Trump, I always was against guns. I didn't want guns. And now since this happened"— it's up in the prison area— "my husband and I are finally in agreement, because he wanted the guns. We now have a gun on every table. We're ready to start shooting."

I said, "Very interesting."

So protect the Second Amendment.

End— end Common Core. Common Core should— it is a disaster. Bush is totally in favor of Common Core. I don't see how he can possibly get the nomination. He's weak on immigration. He's in favor of Common Core. How the hell can you vote for this guy? You just can't do it. We have to end education has to be local.

Rebuild the country's infrastructure.

Nobody can do that like me. Believe me. It will be done on time, on budget, way below cost, way below what anyone ever thought.

I look at the roads being built all over the country, and I say I can build those things for one-third. What they do is unbelievable, how bad.

You know, we're building on Pennsylvania Avenue, the Old Post Office, we're converting it into one of the world's great hotels. It's gonna be the best hotel in Washington, D.C. We got it from the General Services Administration in Washington. The Obama administration. We got it. It was the most highly sought after— or one of them, but I think the most highly sought after project in the history of General Services. We got it. People were shocked, Trump got it.

Well, I got it for two reasons. Number one, we're really good. Number two, we had a really good plan. And I'll add in the third, we had a great financial statement. Because the General Services, who are terrific people, by the way, and talented people, they wanted to do a great job. And they wanted to make sure it got built.

So we have to rebuild our infrastructure, our bridges, our roadways, our airports. You come into La Guardia Airport, it's like we're in a third world country. You look at the patches and the 40-year-old floor. They throw down asphalt, and they throw.

You look at these airports, we are like a third world country. And I come in from China and I come in from Qatar and I come in from different places, and they have the most incredible airports in the world. You come to back to this country and you have LAX, disaster. You have all of these disastrous airports. We have to rebuild our infrastructure.

Save Medicare, Medicaid and Social Security without cuts. Have to do it.

Get rid of the fraud. Get rid of the waste and abuse, but save it. People have been paying it for years. And now many of these candidates want to cut it. You save it by making the United States, by making us rich again, by taking back all of the money that's being lost.

Renegotiate our foreign trade deals.

Reduce our $18 trillion in debt, because, believe me, we're in a bubble. We have artificially low interest rates. We have a stock market that, frankly, has been good to me, but I still hate to see what's happening. We have a stock market that is so bloated.

Be careful of a bubble because what you've seen in the past might be small potatoes compared to what happens. So be very, very careful.

And strengthen our military and take care of our vets. So, so important.

Sadly, the American dream is dead.

But if I get elected president I will bring it back bigger and better and stronger than ever before, and we will make America great again.

Thank you. Thank you very much.

Contact us at <u>editors@time.com</u>.

Appendix 3

Payne Stewart

GOLF; With Smiles and Tears, Stewart's Family and Friends Say Goodbye

By CLIFTON BROWN

OCT. 30, 1999

It was a memorial service that fit the personality of Payne Stewart – emotional, humorous, unique and unforgettable.

More than 3,000 people came to First Baptist Church of Orlando today to pay their respects to Stewart, one of six people who died Monday in a plane crash. In his opening remarks, the Rev. J. B. Collingsworth, the pastor, warned that the service would bring both laughter and tears. He was right, as the 90-minute service reflected on the many sides of Stewart, who lived his 42 years to the fullest, touching people round the world.

Stewart's accomplishments as a golfer were well known to sports fans who watched Stewart win two United States Open championships, a P.G.A. Championship and 18 tournaments worldwide. But those closest to Stewart knew that his family and his faith mattered the most to him. Making her first public appearance since her husband's death, Tracey Stewart spoke at the service, as the couple's daughter and son, 13-year-old Chelsea and 10-year-old Aaron, sat in the church's front row. Tracey Stewart described Payne as a devoted husband and father, as a devout Christian and as someone who could not be replaced in their lives.

''When I met Payne, I thought he was the most beautiful man I had ever seen in my life,'' she said. ''After 18 years of marriage, he was still the most beautiful man I had ever seen, not because of the way he looked on the outside anymore, but because of what he was on the inside.''

More than 100 of the world's most prominent golfers attended the service. Many of them are competing in the Tour Championship in Houston, which was suspended for the day to allow players to attend the service. The Southern Farm Bureau Classic in Madison, Miss., another PGA Tour event, was also suspended. Tiger Woods, Davis Love 3d, Phil Mickelson, Hal Sutton and Justin Leonard were among those who arrived Thursday night from Houston. Others, like Jack Nicklaus, Greg Norman and Fred Couples, traveled from their homes.

''We didn't show up because he was a golfer,'' Brad Faxon said. ''We showed up because he was a special guy.''

At the front of the massive church, many belongings of Stewart's were on display, including his United States Open and P.G.A. Championship trophies, a pair of his trademark knickers and family portraits. His children left more personal artifacts, including a bottle of Rogaine, fake buckteeth and a framed message that said: ''We love you Dad. We will miss you.''

There was a picture of Stewart and Aaron, taken at last week's father-son tournament at the National Car Rental Classic here, the last tournament in which Stewart competed. Stewart missed the cut last week, but that allowed him to watch Aaron play football. Aaron scored a touchdown, and Stewart was there to cheer.

Once the service started, there were musical tributes from the recording artists Michael W. Smith and Vince Gill, who wrote a song this week titled, ''Hey, God,'' in tribute to his friend Stewart.

Several of Stewart's closest friends told intimate stories. Chuck Cook, his golf coach, recalled relaxing at Pebble Beach with Stewart when he was approached by an overbearing fan who questioned Stewart's identity.

'' 'Some guy says that you're Payne Stewart, and I don't believe it,' '' Cook recalled. ''Payne said: 'Suppose I go get the U.S. Open trophy, and you keep filling it up with whatever I want to drink. Will that prove it to you?' ''

Stewart then told the bartender to pour some very expensive champagne, courtesy of the humbled man.

''He may be the only guy I know who was sorry he met Payne Stewart,'' Cook said.

Paul Azinger, the 1993 P.G.A. champion, began his remarks by rolling up his pants into his socks, knickers style, and donning a tam-o'-shanter as people in the church applauded. Azinger then told about Stewart ruining the engine on a fishing boat by starting it while it was still parked in the garage, causing the engine to explode.

''Payne wasn't the most mechanically inclined person I've ever met,'' Azinger said. ''When the engine popped, flames shot up to the ceiling. He almost burned the house down.''

But Azinger soon pulled his pants out of his socks, took off his hat and became serious. Before he could finish his remarks, he was crying.

''Trying to cope with the magnitude of this tragedy is one of the most difficult things I've ever had to do,'' said Azinger, who was also close with two other victims in Monday's crash, Van Ardan and Robert Fraley, Stewart's agents.

Later in the service, Collingsworth instructed members of the church to pass out bracelets to everyone in attendance that were inscribed with the letters W.W.J.D.: What Would Jesus Do. Stewart wore a similar bracelet every day, which was a gift from Aaron. Collingsworth asked the players to wear the bracelets on the golf course when the Tour Championship resumes Saturday in honor of Stewart.

Near the end of the service, a video of Stewart was played on a screen in the front of the church. During the video,

Stewart was shown being interviewed, saying that he knew he was going to a special place when he died.

In the last several years of his life, Stewart's personality changed because of his renewed faith. There were times early in his career when Stewart could be abrupt or surly, particularly when he was not playing well. But after winning the United States Open this year and being part of last month's winning Ryder Cup team, Stewart had never seemed more content.

''Payne said, 'I don't have any more goals,' '' Cook said. '' 'I'm having a hard time getting motivated. I'm so happy. I just want to stay home.' ''

When the service ended, players from the tour lined up along the center aisle of the church, then Stewart's family filed out between them.

''I thought the service was absolutely beautiful,'' said Mets pitcher Orel Hershiser, a friend of Stewart's. ''I'm glad the video wasn't any longer. I couldn't continue to watch, knowing that he's gone.''

Chronicling the Spiritual Journey of 1999 U.S. Open Champion Payne Stewart

To understand golfer Payne Stewart—the most public of sports figures, who died the most public of deaths last October—you have to look deeper to see what changed him over the last 18 months of his life. And the best way to do that is through the eyes of his friends and colleagues.

"The one thing I think about Payne was that he was genuine," says fellow PGA pro David Ogrin.

Ogrin knew Stewart from his college days when David played for Texas A&M and Payne starred for the Southern Methodist University Mustangs. He observed him closely for nearly 20 years and is perhaps one of the best qualified to comment on Stewart's decade-long journey from highly successful yet highly dissatisfied pro golfer to a confident and peaceful belief in Jesus Christ in the last year and a half of his life.

"I knew him when he was the perfect Frat Rat," Ogrin says. "I played against him for three years and knew he was a genuine hard worker. At times he could be a genuine pain in the neck, but we all knew he was a genuine champion. When he talked to you, he was genuinely interested in what you had to say."

But Ogrin, like Stewart's many close friends, including golfer Paul Azinger, sports agent Robert Fraley, and baseball pitcher Orel Hershiser, came to see a genuine difference in the once egotistical and often sarcastic golfer.

"In the last couple of years, Payne became a genuine Christian. He had earned everything a man could earn on his own in the golf world and found that it wasn't enough," Ogrin adds. "To understand what finished out the man and the grasp that it held on him, you have to see what Jesus has to offer and the place He played in Payne's life."

The difference, according to PGA Tour chaplain Larry Moody, was that Stewart went from having a religion he could fall back on if needed, to a personal relationship with Jesus, which carried him through the highs and lows of his final months in this bunker we call "earth."

Moody, who often leads the Wednesday night Tour Bible study, began making the rounds on the PGA Tour in 1981, Stewart's rookie year. He too witnessed first-hand the changes in Stewart's life.

"We had some good talks after his father passed away in the early 90s. Then his good friend Paul Azinger was stricken with cancer in 1993. He had talked to Payne about not being in the land of the living and going to the land of the dying, but actually being in the land of the dying and heading for the land of the living.

"Although Paul was sure where he was going, Payne did not share the same confidence," Moody adds.

All the while, Stewart's agent Fraley and his wife Dixie, along with good friend Van Ardan, were continually talking to him about a relationship with Jesus and how the peace and joy of a personal Savior could overwhelm any golf trophy Stewart would ever win.

The most constant reminder of his need to change inside and out came from his two young children, Chelsea and Aaron. They began attending a Christian sports camp each summer in Missouri, Stewart's home state, and they made sure of their eternal destiny during one of the camps.

"We always said they were raising Payne just like he was raising them," Stewart's longtime golf teacher Chuck Cook says. "They brought home the Christian life and the Christian values to him on a daily basis."

When it came time for Tracey and Payne to select a school for the two kids, the Stewarts sought out one of the top Christian schools near their Orlando, Florida, home, the First Academy at the First Baptist Church of Orlando.

While the denominational label was ultimately unimportant, the teaching Payne received at the church proved to be one of the final mileposts of his spiritual journey.

Stewart began attending a men's Bible study led by major league pitcher Hershiser, who also stressed the need for a personal relationship with God. Orel emphasized that being accepted by God is not based on good works but on faith in Jesus—the One who had paid the penalty for his sins and could make him righteous before a holy God.

"God used a little bit of everybody in Payne's life," says First Baptist associate pastor J.B. Collingsworth. "Larry Moody and Paul Azinger were factors, his kids brought it home to him daily, and he came to First Baptist Orlando, where he joined the men's Bible study and learned many things here."

Stewart also became good friends with golf legend Byron Nelson, one of golf's greatest winners, who told Payne of his own need to have Jesus in his life to help, guide, and comfort him.

"Payne was as solid as they come," Nelson says. "He loved Tracey and the kids, but he had a real love and peace in his life from Christ."

Despite all the shared knowledge and friendly persuasion, Stewart had to settle his spiritual relationship alone, which he did—asking Christ into his life as his personal Savior and Lord privately in 1998.

Shortly after that, Payne's son Aaron helped Dad let the world in on his changed life.

Early in the 1999 golf season, Aaron gave his dad his WWJD bracelet, which stands for "What Would Jesus Do?" The 10-year-old proved wise beyond his years when he challenged Dad to come out of the closet and let others know about his private commitment to Christ.

Moody was one of the first to hear from Payne about his bold commitment when he encountered him on the practice range at the Shell Houston Hope in April. Seeing Stewart wearing the bracelet, Moody asked for some background information and listened as Stewart told him that God had truly changed his mind, body, and spirit.

"In the last year, I knew Payne was committed to God, but in Houston was when I found he was unashamed publicly of his commitment," Moody says.

The rest of the sports world caught on a few months later when Stewart conquered the demanding Pinehurst No. 2 layout to win his second US Open title, capping the victory with a bracelet-encircled fist thrust into the air on the 18th green.

That photo and Stewart's spoken, public commitment were played around the world the following day as his path from carnal, clutter-filled darkness to peaceful life became clear.

Collingsworth, who became a friend of Stewart's over the last 18 months, spoke with Stewart at a post-US Open party thrown last July by his wife to help map out his future path.

"He told me he wasn't going to be a 'Bible thumper;' that wasn't his style. But he wanted everybody to know it was Jesus, Jesus, Jesus who had done this great thing in his life, and that was all-important."

Moody said that in the past Stewart would mock players who attended the weekly Bible study for being less than perfect and even quite human at times.

"I told him only sinners came to the Bible study, and if he wasn't one then he shouldn't show up because he would make the rest of us look bad," Moody says, recalling his tongue-in-check response.

Eventually, of course, Stewart became aware that although he was less than perfect as a player or a person, he was forgiven by the One he had accepted into his life.

For Darin Hoff, who grew up with Stewart in Springfield, Missouri, and who knew Payne since age 15, the change began to come into focus when his buddy lost the US Open title to Lee Janzen in 1998.

"I saw he was truly gracious in defeat and really cheered Lee Janzen when he won. I knew that was not like the old Payne. His faith was so much more important to him than it ever had been before," Hoff says.

Hoff was working as an assistant golf pro in South Bend, Indiana, when he received the stunning news of the death of Stewart, Fraley, Ardan, and the others. Payne's old friend grabbed a flight to Orlando for the memorial service. He spent much of the trip thinking about his friend and the difference he had seen in his life over the last year.

"At the memorial service, I realized that I didn't have what Payne did. It was like God was standing right there calling me to come to Him. My life was changed forever on that day, and I know I will never be the same."

Collingsworth says that in the months since Stewart's death, he has heard from people all over the country who have been affected by it and desire to follow the golfer's spiritual path.

Moody, who has dealt with professional golfers for nearly two decades, can only shake his head in amazement at the pathway Stewart traveled in his professional, private, and spiritual life.

"What a tremendous legacy he has left us. How thrilled we are to know him and to know that his story is attracting so many others to what Payne has found."

It was a winding pathway, but an eternally fulfilling one for the most public of golfers, who made the most public of life-changing commitments. And now all the world is find out about the transformation that made Payne Stewart's life—and death—a tribute to His Savior.

By Art Stricklin

This story was published in the March 2000 issue of Sports Spectrum.

CPSIA information can be obtained
at www.ICGtesting.com
Printed in the USA
BVHW060957080721
611457BV00022B/873